Kate Webb

PROVERBS

FOR LIFE!

Learn the Bible Keys For a Better You!

By Barry L. Davis, D.Min.

Copyright©2013 Barry L. Davis

GodSpeed Publishing

Visit Us for More Great Resources at:
www.amazon.com/author/barrydavis
www.pastorshelper.com

All rights reserved. No part of this book may be reproduced in any form, except for the inclusion of brief quotations in reviews, without permission in writing from the author/publisher.

Unless otherwise indicated, all Scripture quotations are taken from the *Holy Bible,* New Living Translation, copyright © 1996, 2004. Used by permission of Tyndale House Publishers, Inc., Wheaton, Illinois 60189. All rights reserved.

Scripture quotations marked NRSV are from the **New Revised Standard Version Bible**, copyright © 1989 National Council of the Churches of Christ in the United States of America. Used by permission. All rights reserved.

Scripture quotations marked MSG are taken from **The Message**. Copyright © 1993, 1994, 1995, 1996, 2000, 2001, 2002. Used by permission of NavPress Publishing Group."

Table of Contents

Key #1: HOW TO GAIN WISDOM — 7

Key #2: HOW TO ACHIEVE YOUR GOALS — 21

Key #3: HOW TO HAVE A HAPPY HOME — 33

Key #4: HOW TO BE PERSONALLY DISCIPLINED — 45

Key #5: HOW TO CHOOSE THE RIGHT FRIENDS — 59

Key #6: HOW TO OVERCOME PRIDE — 71

Key #7: HOW TO GUARD AGAINST GOSSIP — 83

Key #8: HOW TO EXPERIENCE PROSPERITY — 95

THANK YOU FOR INVESTING IN THIS BOOK! — 107

7-8:30
12 weeks Heather

Key #1: HOW TO GAIN WISDOM

Have you ever heard of the Darwin Awards? They are awards that are given each year to people who make really, really, really bad choices in life. Let me share a couple of recent ones with you:

> [1](28 May 2004, Italy) Fabio, 28, left the family ostrich business for a new job as a truck driver. But his interests were more eclectic than the average ostrich-farming truck driver. Relaxing one evening with friends at a pub in Cursi, Fabio shifted the conversation to his new interest in spy gadgets. He pulled an ordinary-looking pen out of his pocket and explained that it was actually a single-shot pistol. To demonstrate, he pointed it at his head and clicked the button. The cleverly disguised gadget worked perfectly, sending a .22-caliber bullet into Fabio's left occipital lobe.

---

[1] **www.darwinawards.com**

(29 April 2004, Brushy Fork, WV) Alfred, 63, had trouble with termites at home. He had heard that natural gas was dangerous, and figured it would be a good, low-cost way to fumigate his house. So he shut the doors and windows, turned on the gas, and spent the night in a nearby camper trailer with his wife. The next morning he stepped out of the trailer, took a breath of the crisp, cool air, and strode over to his house. When he opened the door, the slight spark from the latch ignited the cloud of natural gas that had accumulated in his home. The force of the explosion blew him off the porch and into a nearby creek, knocked out the town's telephones and electricity, and blew the doors off a church. It rattled windows and nerves six miles away. Alfred was evacuated by helicopter with severe burns to the burn unit at the Cabell-Huntington Hospital. His house was uninsured – It is presumed that the fumigation was effective.

I'm afraid these guys had not taken advantage of God's promise:

> *If any of you is lacking in wisdom, <u>ask God</u>, who gives to all generously and ungrudgingly, and it will be given you.* – James 1:5 (NRSV)

WHAT IS WISDOM?

Before I get to the definitions I think we need to understand what wisdom is not – wisdom is not intelligence, and it is not age, and it is not wealth. We all know people who are smart, old, or rich who make very foolish choices. So let me give you a couple basic definitions:

> **1. The ability to discern what is true, right, or lasting, and act accordingly.**
> **2. The opposite of foolishness.**

The book of Proverbs makes it clear that wisdom is something we should not only pursue, but we have a promise from God that if we are willing, He will make us wise people.

> *Wisdom shouts in the streets. She cries out in the public square. She calls out to the crowds along the main street, and to those in front of city hall. "You simpletons!" she cries. "How long will*

> *you go on being simpleminded? How long will you mockers relish your mocking? How long will you fools fight the facts? <u>Come here and listen to me! I'll pour out the spirit of wisdom upon you and make you wise</u>.*
> – Proverbs 1:20-23

I believe we all want to be wise people, and make wise choices so the question before us is:

HOW DO I BECOME A WISE PERSON?

Before I give you the answers, I need to stress how humbling it is to write to you on a subject like this – I, like you, am continually working in this area, and while I've acquired some wisdom along the way, I've certainly got a long way to go – but these are the truths I've discovered.

1. UNDERSTAND WISDOM'S VALUE

If I truly value something, I will do whatever it takes to bring it into my possession. Now if you don't value wisdom, nothing I say is going to make much difference to you, but if you understand the value of wisdom you will start acting upon these things right away.

> *Happy is the person who finds wisdom and gains understanding. For the profit of <u>wisdom is better than silver, and <u>her wages are better than gold</u>. <u>Wisdom is more precious than rubies;</u> nothing you desire can compare with her. She offers you life in her right hand, and riches and honor in her left.*
> – Proverbs 3:13-16

You can have a fantastic stock portfolio, and beautiful home, and be the envy of all your friends and family, but if you continually make foolish choices, you will never live a life of satisfaction and joy. Think about some of the most famous people out there today: people like Paris Hilton, or Howard Stern, or some of the others who are so popular in our culture. I would bet money that most of them are not people who value wisdom. And the reason I know this is because although they have all of the material goods a person could desire, they consistently make foolish choices.

Do you know when I decided to pursue wisdom? It was after I discovered that I was making one foolish choice after another. Most of us don't begin placing the appropriate value on wisdom, until we've made fools of ourselves time and time again. It is when we're young and we finally realize the reason we keep getting fired is because we don't show up on time for work – or the reason we can't build up a relationship is because we've refused to remain monogamous – or that we keep bouncing checks because we haven't yet realized that an abundance of checks in our checkbook doesn't equate to lots of money in the bank to cover them. God clearly says that wisdom is of the utmost value – once you and I learn that, we will be well on our way to acquiring the wisdom God offers us.

2. HAVE A HEALTHY FEAR OF GOD

> [2]Haider Sediqi didn't give much thought to the zippered pouch that a passenger forgot in his taxicab when he got out at Los Angeles International Airport. Sediqi stashed the brown bag in the front, where it remained as he took his cab to the car wash, drove a passenger to Long Beach, and met a fellow cabbie for lunch. As he walked off to the restroom, Sediqi asked his friend to check the bag for identification. Inside, packed in clear plastic cases, were about 100 diamonds,

---

[2] *Star-Telegram, www.dfw.com (11-19-05)*

together worth about $350,000 – Also inside was a cell phone bill. Sediqi, 40, a father of two with a pregnant wife, called the number and talked to the man, identified as Eric Austein. He had not yet departed for New York, and they arranged to meet at the airport police station. Police inventoried the diamonds and confirmed Austein's identity. Austein took the gems, hugged Sediqi, and promised him a reward. Sediqi said keeping the loot never entered his mind, even though his wife loves diamonds. "God is up there," he said. "He always watches."

I think that is something we all need to remember as we live our lives. It is not as if we live in fear of God, in the sense that we are afraid He is going to strike us down, or as if He is just waiting for us to mess up. But we should fear Him in the sense that we have the greatest amount of respect for Him and what He thinks, and what He desires for us.

> *Fear of the LORD is the beginning of wisdom. Knowledge of the Holy One results in understanding.*
> – Proverbs 9:10

Isn't it interesting that the Proverb writer says that fear is the beginning point? If we want to be wise, we first have to recognize that God is real, and that God watches over us, and that God is over all, is all powerful, and that He is the Creator. We need to acknowledge every single day that He is God and we are not.

Until we really understand the reality of God's presence both in our world and in our lives, we will not begin to grow in wisdom. But when we see Him as He is, and begin to follow Him as the One who really knows the way, we will have taken the first step toward wisdom. It really comes down to the concept of "reverence" – which means to have a profound awe, respect, and love for God. Once you have that, the rest begins to fall into place.

3. SEEK WISE COUNSEL

I remember vividly when I was younger thinking that I didn't need any one to tell me how to do anything. This was especially true when it came to my parents, and I'm sure many of you had the same experience. Isn't it amazing how those same people who seemed to not have a clue when you were 17 became so wise when you turned 30? While not all of us had wise parents, fortunately many of us did, and we can either go to them now, or reflect on their memories and get wise advice.

The older I get the more I recognize my need for help in this area. Perhaps it is simply getting knocked down enough times when I tried to do things on my own, or maybe it just comes with age, but I am much quicker to seek out wise counsel today than I ever have been at any other time in my life.

> *Fools think they need no advice, but the wise listen to others.*
> – Proverbs 12:15

The problem is, until we recognize that this is true, we will remain fools. Let me get real practical with you for a second – we all need someone, or perhaps a number of people, who we can go to and receive wise counsel. One way to do that is to begin to build friendships with people who have made wise decisions in their own lives – now many times these are going to be people who are older than you who have lots of life experience. There is something to say for someone who has already dealt with life's troubles, and who has already walked down the path you're walking down right now. And who made the "Right godly" decision.

> *Whoever walks with the wise will become wise; whoever walks with fools will suffer harm.* – Proverbs 13:20

Take a good look at the people you spend the most time with – are they building you up, or are they dragging you down? Are they helping to lift you to a new level, or are they a negative influence? Who you spend time with is going to affect you forever.

> *Get all the advice and instruction you can, and be wise the rest of your life.* – Proverbs 19:20

If you don't know someone right now, begin reading books written by wise people who give good advice, or start listening to CDs with good instruction. I am constantly listening to CDs by wise teachers like Stephen Covey, and John Maxwell, and Bill Hybels and others, because I know that I need someone wiser than me to teach me.

Also, start reading your Bible every day – in fact, why not read a part of the Proverbs each day and see what kind of wisdom you can find in this book. God leaves it up to you to spend your life acting the fool, or growing in wisdom. It is entirely your decision to make – God will supply the resources, if you'll supply the willingness to act.

4. LEARN HUMILITY

[3]On March 5, 2005, German long jumper Bianca Kappler created a stir in the world of indoor track and field. Plaudits abounded for Kappler on that day, not for her gold-medal jump, but because she refused the award. Kappler's final jump was measured at 22 feet, 10 inches. The next best contender was Naide Gomes of Portugal. Gomes' jump of 21 feet, 11¾ inches made her a distant second. However, when Kappler was handed the gold, she promptly handed it back, saying, "I know I can't jump that far." When officials asked her to reconsider or take a final jump the next day, Kappler declined. She insisted that her best jumps were nearly a foot shorter than that "medal-winning" effort. Judges concluded her jump must have been measured incorrectly. Kappler ended up with a share of the bronze medal,

---

[3] *"German Athlete Protests Winning Gold," The Associated Press (3-5-05)*

prompting several newspapers to dub her "the world's most honest athlete."

I admire Kappler, not just for her honesty, but for her understanding of what her abilities presently are. In our lives we need to be able to admit to God that we do not have it altogether – to be able to plead ignorance before Him in different areas of our lives – and to have an honest evaluation of where we are at and where we need to be spiritually.

> *Pride leads to disgrace, but with humility comes wisdom.*
> – Proverbs 11:2

It is only when I admit that I am broken that I can be healed. When you can say to God, "I'm not all I can be, and I'm not all I should be, but I desire nothing more than to have you show me the way" – that is when wisdom will begin to flow through your life and the lives of those you influence.

You know what? I never want to be one of the people listed in the Darwin awards. And I don't want to be one of those people who lives my life in foolishness, when all the time God is waiting to pour out His wisdom into my life. I hope that you feel the same today – are you willing to commit yourself to the path of wisdom, beginning right now? Why don't we do it together?

Key #2: HOW TO ACHIEVE YOUR GOALS

Let me begin by asking you a question: When you set out on a trip, do you just load up the car and start driving? Do you go to the airport and buy a ticket on the next available flight, no matter where it's going? Probably not – There's no telling where you might end up, and it could be someplace you really don't want to be.

Your destination is your goal. If you're feeling hungry for great barbeque, you want to go Kansas City. But if you want to enjoy the view from the top of the Empire State Building, you'd best head for The Big Apple.

Success in life, spiritual and otherwise, is every bit as much a destination as is a physical place. Now if you want to reach that destination, you need to know what that destination is, and then you need to have a plan for how to get there. That is what we mean when we talk about setting and <u>achieving goals.</u>

In this book, *Proverbs for Life*, we are discovering what the book of Proverbs has to say about different areas of our life and how, using those Proverbs, we can change our lives for the better. One area that most of us need help is in learning how to achieve our goals. And while the word "goals" is never used in Proverbs, the concept most definitely is, as we shall see.

WHY SET GOALS AT ALL?

I have spoken to people who are opposed to the concept of goals – especially religious people, who seem to think that it is somehow unspiritual. Yet the book of Proverbs gives us some very good reasons for doing this.

(narrow path)

> *My child, don't lose sight of good planning and insight. Hang on to them, for they fill you with life and bring you honor and respect. They keep you safe on your way and keep your feet from stumbling.*
> – Proverbs 3:21-23

It is quite obvious that God wants us to make plans for the future, and wants us to follow those plans until our goals are reached. If you are a spiritual person, I think it is even more important to set and achieve goals than if you were not – let me give you some reasons:

1. IT'S A MATTER OF STEWARDSHIP

We are given one lifetime, and we need to make the most of it while we can. If I am going to be a good steward of the time that God has given me on earth I am going to use that time to accomplish as much as I can. When I set a goal, and then take the steps toward reaching it, I am making wise use of my time and accomplishing much more than I could have otherwise.

I'm not talking about just in the area of work, I'm talking about using time in the best possible way – this includes time for your family, relaxation, and other needs.

When we set goals that are financial, spiritual, and recreational, we will find that we will be able to enjoy more of those things than we ever have before.

> *Take a lesson from the ants, you lazybones. Learn from their ways and be wise! Even though they have no prince, governor, or ruler to make them work, they labor hard all summer, gathering food for the winter.*
> – Proverbs 6:6-8

If the ants know how to be good stewards or their time, surely we can too.

2. IT'S A MATTER OF MEASUREMENT

I don't know about you, but I like to be able to measure my progress. Let's say that I set a goal to read through the New Testament portion of the Bible in the next year. I count up the chapters and discover that there are 260 of them. So I divide 260 by 52 weeks in a year and find out I only need to read five chapters per week to finish the New Testament in one year – so I could read just one chapter a day, Monday – Friday and I would accomplish my goal. But each day as I read, I'm going to check off that chapter and be able to see that I am making progress toward my ultimate goal – it is very motivating.

This same principle is true if I'm investing money, or wanting to spend quality time with my family, or working toward a college degree. Because I have a set plan, and ultimate destination, I am able to measure my progress and discover that my goal is definitely reachable.

3. IT'S A MATTER OF PROSPERITY

This is true in all areas, but it is especially true if I'm setting financial or work-related goals.

> *Good planning and hard work lead to prosperity, but hasty shortcuts lead to poverty.* – Proverbs 21:5

If you want to get ahead in life, you are going to have to set goals, and then work hard to reach them. Notice that the Proverbs writer stipulates that it is "good planning" and "hard work" together that lead to prosperity – you can't have one without the other. If you want to have a better income than you have now, you have to plan and work for it – there is nothing wrong with that, as long as we keep it all in perspective.

WHAT KIND OF GOALS SHOULD I SET?

As I said, you can set goals for work, for investing, for your family, for education, for weight loss, and just about any area of life that you need to plan for. And while I don't think there is any limit as to what kind of goals you should set, I think that as a Christian, they should at least follow these three guidelines.

1. GOALS THAT HONOR GOD

Any goal that is unethical in any way, or keeps you from following God with integrity is a goal that you need to get rid of.

> *Commit your work to the LORD, and then your plans will succeed.*
> – Proverbs 16:3

Our plans and goals should be made in the context of our commitment to God. So no matter what my goal is, it needs to pass the *God Test* before I begin implementing it into my life. I need to be able to ask and answer the following questions in the affirmative:

1) Can I honestly ask God's help in striving to reach this goal?

Is there anything I'm planning that I would not be able to pray for God's assistance with? Is there anything about it that would embarrass me before God?

2) Will I be a better person for accomplishing this goal?

In the process of reaching this goal, and in the accomplishment of it, will I be a better father or mother, a better student, a better businessman, a better son or daughter? Is there something inherently good about what I am doing that will help me develop character, integrity, honesty, and those types of things?

> [4] "Our greatest fear should not be of failure, but of succeeding at

---

[4] New Tribes Missionary (author unknown), Eternal Perspectives Newsletter (Fall 2003), p. 15

> something that doesn't really matter."

2. GOALS THAT ARE S.M.A.R.T[5]

> "The reason most people never reach their goals is that they don't define them, or ever seriously consider them as believable or achievable. Winners can tell you where they are going, what they plan to do along the way, and who will be sharing the adventure with them." – Denis Waitly

I think he is exactly right – and if our goals fit into the S.M.A.R.T. acrostic, they are ones that we will certainly be able to accomplish with God's help.

Specific – a general goal would be, "I'm going to be financially successful" – a specific goal would be, "I'm going to learn how to effectively market an educational product I've developed by taking Course 401 at the local community college next month."

---

[5] Adapted From Paul J. Meyer's "Attitude Is Everything" and other sources.

To set a specific goal you must answer the six "W" questions:

*Who: Who is involved?
*What: What do I want to accomplish?
*Where: Identify a location.
*When: Establish a time frame.
*Which: Identify requirements & constraints.
*Why: Specific reasons, purpose or benefits of accomplishing the goal.

Measurable – We've talked about this already, but we need to make sure that we have goals that allow us to determine whether we are making progress. You should be able to ask questions of your goal like, "How much" "How many" and "How will I know when it is going to be accomplished?" and the answers should be readily available. A good thing to remember is, "If I can't measure it, I can't manage it."

Attainable – When you identify goals that are most important to you, you begin to figure out ways you can make them come true. You develop the attitudes, abilities, skills, and when necessary, the financial capacity to reach them. You begin seeing previously overlooked opportunities to bring yourself closer to the achievement of your goals. You can attain most any goal you set when you plan your steps wisely and establish a time frame that allows you to carry out those steps. Goals that may have seemed far away and out of reach eventually move closer and become attainable, not because your goals shrink, but because you grow and expand to match them. When you list your goals you begin to develop the traits and personality that allows you to possess them.

Realistic – To be realistic, a goal must represent an objective toward which you are both *willing* and *able* to work. A goal can be both high and realistic; you are the only one who can decide just how high your goal should be. But be sure that every goal represents substantial progress. A high goal is frequently easier to reach than a low one because a low goal exerts low motivational force. Some of the hardest jobs you ever accomplished actually seem easy simply because they were a labor of love. Your goal is probably realistic if you truly *believe* that it can be accomplished. But if you say that your goal is to read through the Bible every single day of your life, you are not being realistic at all. And when you set unrealistic goals, you're just setting yourself up for a letdown.

Timely – Set a timeframe for the goal: for next week, in three months, by fifth grade – whatever your goal is, it needs to have a beginning and an ending point. Putting an end point on your goal gives you a clear target to work towards. If you don't set a time, the commitment is too vague. It tends not to happen because you feel you can start at any time. Without a time limit, there's no urgency to start taking action now.

3. GOALS I'M WILLING TO PAY THE PRICE FOR

When your goals fit into the criteria we've mentioned so far, you will be blessed, God will be blessed, and the people around you will be blessed. But we need to understand that there is a price to be paid to these goals. If the goal is a good one, the price paid will be well worth it. If I'm going to climb up the corporate ladder, I am going to have to work very hard, improve myself in any number of areas, and consistently gain new skills and abilities. If my goal is further education, I am going to have to study hard, pay for my tuition, and be willing to devote a large portion of my life to school.

Those are good goals that cost a lot, but the benefits are usually worth it if we keep God as the director of all that we say and do. But then there are those all-important spiritual goals that we should be setting. The Apostle Paul set some goals for his life that were of a spiritual nature:

> *I want to know Christ and the power of his resurrection and the sharing of his sufferings by becoming like him in his death, if somehow I may attain the resurrection from the dead.*
> – Philippians 3:10-11 (NRSV)

Now the first part of Paul's goal is something many people could align themselves with – "to know Christ and the power of His resurrection." But another part of his goal was "the sharing of (Jesus') sufferings by becoming like him in his death." Paul felt that to fully identify with Christ, he needed not only to share in His power and glory, but also share in His suffering. And that is exactly what he did throughout his ministry – share in the sufferings of Christ. That was the price he was willing to pay.

Some of life's goals lead us to share in that same type of price, and for others, it is a cost not quite so great – but there is always a cost. If we are going to be achievers in any area of life, we must be willing to do, say, and experience whatever is necessary to reach our goals. Sometimes the experience of paying the price shapes us more than the reaching of the goal.

I hope that you've decided to set some goals today. Perhaps you've decided to learn how to be a better parent, and you're going to take the steps necessary to reach that goal. Or maybe you're going to make a decision to go back to school and finish what you've started. Or perhaps you've decided that your prayer life isn't what it should be, and you're going to begin spending at least 15 minutes in prayer every day beginning today. Whatever your goal, make sure to allow God to be the main motivation for whatever you decide to do, and you can't go wrong.

Key #3: HOW TO HAVE A HAPPY HOME

It doesn't take a degree in sociology to recognize that America and the rest of the world can no longer be considered a "Leave It To Beaver" society. In the last 40 years the family in our society has taken some hard knocks.

Let me tell you some of the dramatic changes that have taken place since 1960 in the USA:

*There has been a 400% increase in the divorce rate and a 200% increase in the number of children who are raised in single-parent homes.

*Today 70% of preschool-aged children have mothers who work outside the home, and 80% of school-aged children come home each day to an empty house.

Needless to say, these numbers were significantly less in 1960.

A couple of years ago Newsweek printed an article on the 21st century family, and began by saying, "The American family does not exist. Rather, we creating new American families of diverse style and shapes in unprecedented numbers."

Here's a statistic that might surprise you. We normally refer to the "traditional family" as one mom, one dad, one marriage, and children from that marriage only. However, today only 1 out of 6 people in America fit into that category. The other 83% come a variety of other situations. The traditional American family is no longer the typical American family. As I said, it doesn't take a social psychologist to recognize that the deterioration of the traditional family has taken its toll on the emotional well-being of millions of children.

In 1946, a poll was taken of high school teachers, asking them to name the top offenses their students committed. They were: - **talking – chewing gum – making noises – running in the halls – getting out of turn in line – wearing improper clothing and – not putting paper in the waste basket.** You can tell these teenagers were out of control!

Sixty years later what do you think the top offenses committed by teenagers are? In order, – **rape – robbery – assault – burglary – arson – murder – suicide.** As you can see, we have our work cut out for us.

The question is, how can we have happy, biblically functioning homes in a world like ours? – Thankfully, the book of Proverbs helps us out in this area.

1. ESTABLISH A STRONG MARRIAGE

Before I say anything else, I know that some of you are divorced, some might be separated, and others might be having huge struggles in their marriage. What I'm going to say is not meant to offend or condemn, but simply to convey what the ideal situation is from a biblical standpoint on having a happy home-life. If you are not in that ideal situation, please at least try to take the principles I'm going to share and do your best to adapt them to your personal circumstances. Let me give you several ways to establish a strong marriage.

1) STAY CAPTIVATED

Now men, I need to warn you that I'm about to quote a Bible verse that has the word "breasts" in it – I'm telling you this ahead of time so you won't get so caught up in the thought that you'll miss the rest of the passage.

> <u>*Let your wife be a fountain of blessing for you*</u>. *Rejoice in the wife of your youth. She is a loving doe, a graceful deer. Let her breasts satisfy you always.* <u>*May you always be captivated by her love*</u>. – Proverbs 5:18-19

I realize that this is speaking of husbands to wives, but the principle is the same regardless. He says, "May you always be captivated by her love." Instead of "captivated" the KJV says, "ravished," the NASB says, "exhilarated," the NKJV says, "enraptured," and the NRSV says, "intoxicated."

Here is what I think this is saying: Find the joyful aspect of your relationship with your spouse and revel in that joy, whatever it is – find the common interest, the passions, and engage in them. Lean into whatever dimension of your marriage relationship provides a mutual sense of exhilaration.

How long has it been since you've looked at your husband or wife and felt that exhilaration you felt when you were first seeing each other? While we all change physically, and in many other ways as we grow older, we need to remember to continually focus on what is attractive in our spouse. And I'm not talking about looks, though that might be part of it – I'm talking about those inner qualities that attracted you to him or her in the first place.

2) STAY TOGETHER

The Bible is clear that the marriage relationship is to be permanent and the bedrock foundation for families to be built on. We can never forge strong families; we can't improve the basic building block of society without the establishment and development of permanent, satisfying marriages. The only kind of marriage that the writer of Proverbs understands is a lifelong marriage.

The writer of Proverbs would patiently listen to all of today's banter about no-fault divorces, serial marriages, divorces and remarriages, spouse trading every six or eight years and when all the chatter ceased, he would repeat his mantra we just read: "Rejoice in the spouse of your youth."

When you get married, stay together – Work it out–Make compromises–Get help. Talk, pray, try and try and try again, but stay together if at all possible. I know that sometimes there are extenuating circumstances, but if at all possible, stick this thing out and work it through. Make the most out of your marriage because strong families flow out of solid marriage relationships – relationships that last till death do us part.

3) STAY FAITHFUL

[6]In the 2005 movie *Hitch*, Will Smith plays a guy who wins fame as a relationship expert. In real life, Will is married to actress Jada Pinkett Smith. His philosophy on marriage in real life, may remove him from the top of your marriage-consultant list. The Smiths, advocate what might be called therapeutic adultery – adultery within certain rules. To begin with, there's the spousal notification rule. As Will explained to the New York Post, "In our marriage vows, we didn't say 'forsaking all others.' The vow we made was that "you will never hear of something I did after the fact." Then there's the spousal consent rule. "If it came down to it, " Will says, "then one (spouse) can say to the other, 'Look, I need to have sex with somebody. I'm not going to if you don't approve of it — but please approve of it."

---

[6] *Citizen Magazine (May 2005), p. 14*

> *The man who commits adultery is an utter fool, for he destroys his own soul. Wounds and constant disgrace are his lot. His shame will never be erased.* – Proverbs 6:32

How much more straight-forward can you get than that? The writer of Proverbs says just don't do it! Take it off the radar screen of options in your mind – Make it out of the question. He says adultery is such an utterly destructive activity, that those who engage in it are "utter fools." They destroy themselves with guilt and shame. And worse, they'll probably destroy their spouse and family, and probably take another family down with them as well. It's a loser all the way around – The writer says just don't even think about it. In fact, it is such a huge issue, that it is the only activity where Jesus says divorce can be justified.

And you know what? On a practical note, I've never met one person who gave into temptation and committed adultery and was later glad about doing it. Rather, they live the rest of their lives with the guilt and shame of breaking the promise that they made to their spouse and to God. It is throwing everything away for a moment of pleasure. Eventually the words come out, "I have wrecked everything because of what I've done. I have wrecked everything." Almost every time, they will also add, "Oh, if I could only turn the clock back! If I could only have a do-over! If I could only go back and make a different choice."

Anything that threatens or imperils a marriage, anything that could potentially undermine a marriage should be looked at very carefully. There should be no naiveté regarding the power of temptation or the power of seduction, even in a strong marriage.

> *If you think you are standing strong, be careful, for you, too, may fall into the same sin.* – 1 Corinthians 10:12

Remember this – When you get married, marry carefully because you're marrying permanently. And build the marriage to its fullest potential. Now, once a solid marriage is in place we have the challenge of raising children if God blesses us with them.

2. ADOPT EFFECTIVE PARENTING PRACTICES

There is going to come a day when you don't have to remind your child to clean his room, or to eat all her vegetables, or to pick up after themselves. Because one of those days that child is going to be out of your house. While it might not seem like it to you right now, you have a limited amount of time with your kids. So we need to make sure that we do the best we can as parents now.

1) VIEW YOUR KIDS AS A GIFT FROM GOD

That precious child you have in your possession has been given to you as a gift, and you need to treat him or her as the most precious gift you've ever received. Whether you gave birth to them, or adopted them, they have been given to you by God's grace and you are responsible for caring for them in the best way possible.

2) VIEW YOUR KIDS AS ADULTS IN THE MAKING

That child that has been given to me from God will one day be an adult. How I care for them today will have a huge effect on who they will be tomorrow. There are two particular aspects we need to pay attention to: love and discipline. Thankfully, one verse in Proverbs brings these two concepts together:

> *If you refuse to discipline your children, it proves you don't love them; if you love your children, you will be prompt to discipline them.* – Proverbs 13:24

Just as God disciplines those He loves, we discipline the children that He has given to us to help them to become the adults He wants them to become. Discipline takes many forms, but in particular when they are little, physical discipline is necessary – and yes, I said "necessary."

> *Don't fail to correct your children. They won't die if you spank them. Physical discipline may well save them from death.* – Proverbs 23:13-14

If you do not discipline your kids, according to the Bible, you do not love them. And I hope we all know there is a huge difference between discipline and abuse, but discipline must take place if you want your kids to turn out okay.

3) VIEW YOUR KIDS AS LITTLE "YOUS"

It's easy to look into the faces of our kids and see the physical resemblance there, but we need to keep in mind that when they grow up they are going to reflect their Moms and Dads internally. And while they have free choice as to what they will do when they get older and can make decisions that are outside the realm of what they have been taught, we need to do the best we can to be a model of what we want them to become.

> *The godly walk with integrity; blessed are their children after them.*
> – Proverbs 20:7

The blessing he is talking about is that they will very likely follow the example of integrity that you have set. But it is also true if we do not live lives of integrity – can we expect our children to do any better than the example we have set? In many ways, our children are a mirror of ourselves.

> *Teach your children to choose the right path, and when they are older, they will remain upon it.* – Proverbs 22:6

While this is not a promise that children will keep the faith of their parents, it is a general statement of truth that most likely they will. Some start on the right path, and stay on it. Others start on the right path, walk away from it, and then come back. And then others start on the right path, walk away from it, and never return.

We cannot control the decisions that our children make as they get older, but we can set the best example possible in the here and now so that the likelihood of them sticking with the faith will be much higher than if we did not.

So that's it! Establish a strong marriage and work on effective parenting practices and you will have a happy home. A perfect home? No – A home that never has any problems? No. But you will have a home that honors God and has the best chance of being successful in a world that appears to be doing everything it can to destroy the family.

Key #4: HOW TO BE PERSONALLY DISCIPLINED

I imagine many of you follow the Olympics on TV every couple of years. Every time the Olympics come around I am absolutely amazed at the pure athleticism that is displayed at the different events. One competitor after another lines up, and demonstrates a level of skill that is far beyond what any of us would be capable of doing. We are able to witness the muscles that have been developed for a specific sport, the focus of people who know exactly what they are there for, and the poise of a determined athlete. What we are watching is the end result of many years of training that comes from a person who is so disciplined that they have laid everything on the line to become the best they can possibly be in their particular event.

While I would venture to guess that none of us have the physical discipline of an Olympic athlete, we are called to a discipline that in the grand scheme of things, is much more important.

> *...Spend your time and energy in training yourself for <u>spiritual fitness</u>. Physical exercise has some value, but <u>spiritual exercise is much more*</u>

> *important, for it promises a reward in both this life and the next.*
> – 1 Timothy 4:7b-8

As we begin this chapter of *Proverbs for Life*, I want us to focus on what Proverbs tells us about personal discipline. And while the principles we look at can apply to any area of our lives, I especially want to focus on the spiritual disciplines – things like prayer, Bible reading, fasting, and this type of thing.

What I am talking about is becoming a fine-tuned, highly disciplined person, when it comes to developing yourself into the person God wants you to become. Just like an athlete needs to work out his/her body in a certain way to be able to compete physically, we need to work our spirits in such a way that makes us more attuned to God and His direction for our lives.

1. RAISE YOUR STANDARDS HIGHER

What expectations do you have for yourself when it comes to your relationship with God? What do you expect in regard to your prayer life? What do you expect in regard to your time in God's Word? If your expectations are low, most likely you will achieve very little. The fact is that most people have very low standards in these areas. Consider the Bible – the Bible is God's revelation of Himself to human kind, but sadly, even most Christians are highly illiterate when it comes to God's Word.

> *"Americans revere the Bible - but, by and large, they don't read it. And because they don't read it, they have become a nation of biblical illiterates."*
> - George Gallup and Jim Castelli

Consider these results from recent surveys by George Barna:
*Fewer than half of all adults can name the four gospels.
*Many professing Christians cannot identify more than two or three of the disciples.
*60% of Americans can't name even five of the Ten Commandments.
*82% of Americans believe *God helps those who help themselves* is a Bible verse.
*12% of adults believe that Joan of Arc was Noah's wife.
*A survey of graduating high school seniors revealed that over 50% thought that Sodom and Gomorrah were husband and wife.
*A considerable number of respondents to one poll indicated that the Sermon on the Mount was preached by Billy Graham.

-- "Increasingly, America is biblically illiterate." - George Barna

Obviously, we have some big problems to overcome, and it starts with us as individuals raising the standard of personal expectation. At some level, you can usually gauge how much spiritual success you will attain, by what your expectations are going in.

In my experience most of us set our expectations way too low, and those low expectations lead to a life that is not lived in the fullness of God. So my question to you today is this – do you really want to draw closer to God? Do you really desire to be in a dynamic relationship with Him? If so, then you need to raise your personal standard – how much time are you willing to devote to your time with God? If it's five minutes per day, then don't expect to grow very much, if it is one hour, then you can expect much more.

It isn't as if time spent with God is the only factor, but I'm using that as an example of how our personal dedication to God will be reflected in how much more knowledgeable about Him we will grow, and how much closer to Him we will be. We have to dedicate ourselves to cherish every moment we have with God's Word, and every minute we spend with Him in prayer. Only when we raise that standard of expectation will we be ready to acquire the discipline necessary.

> *To acquire wisdom is to love oneself; <u>people who cherish understanding</u> will prosper.* – Proverbs 19:8

The most important understanding that we will ever have is our understanding of God, our relationship with Him, and our place in this world. And what I am asking you to do today is to dedicate yourself to raising the bar of expectation in your spiritual life.

If right now you are spending zero time with God in prayer, raise the bar to 10 minutes or 20 minutes per day – if you're spending 20 minutes it, raise it to 30. If you are reading none of the Bible right now, why not read 2 chapters a day? If you're reading 2 chapters now, why not bump it up to 4 or 5? Begin searching for ways to increase the time you spend with God, as well as the quality of that time, just like you would in building a relationship with your spouse.

Also, are you taking advantage of the opportunities in your area that are offered for growth? Are you attending a Sunday School class, small group, or perhaps attending a Bible study, or book club? All of these are designed to help you raise the standard in your spiritual life.

> *Intelligent people are always open to new ideas. In fact, they look for them.* – Proverbs 18:15

What ideas have you been open to in raising the bar in your time with God? If you haven't been open, don't worry about what you haven't done in the past; instead, start planning now on how you will raise the bar in the future.

2. ACCEPT DELAYED GRATIFICATION

Now what I'm about to tell you is probably going to go against your nature, because we live in a society that expects, and receives, instant gratification in almost every area of life. We have microwave popcorn, online banking, downloadable books, MP3 music files, e-mail, plastic surgery, pay-per-view movies, and the list goes on and on.

We are used to having almost every desire in our lives satisfied within seconds. Even my dog expects instant gratification – we give him a dog biscuit when he comes in from going to the bathroom outside – and if he doesn't get it right away, he will follow you around until you give it to him – our old dog used to bark at us.

But the truth of the matter is, the best things in life are the things that we have to work toward, and wait for.

> *Hope deferred makes the heart sick, but when dreams come true, there is life and joy.* – Proverbs 13:12

The fact of the matter is, you might raise your personal standard, and start spending more and better time with God, and not notice a huge difference right away. And some people get real disappointed because they don't think things are happening fast enough, so they just give up and go back to their old habits. The sad thing is, they might have been a few days or weeks away from a spiritual breakthrough that they never experienced, because they didn't understand the blessing of delayed gratification.

We have to be disciplined enough that we are willing to wait for the blessings to come our way and do the day-to-day things that are necessary for that to happen. You don't become an Olympic athlete overnight – it takes daily discipline in conditioning, diet, personal training, and so forth. And you don't become a spiritual giant overnight – it is the daily routine of prayer, Bible reading, and thinking upon the things of God that will eventually lead you to a position of spiritual strength and vitality. And the truth of the matter is, sometimes it's hard and you don't feel like doing it.

No discipline is enjoyable while it is happening – it is painful! But afterward there will be a quiet harvest of right living for those who are trained in this way. – Hebrews 12:11

If you are willing to wait for the blessing, you will be well on your way to being a personally disciplined individual.

3. FOCUS ON YOUR HEART, MIND, AND ACTIONS

There are many areas of our lives where we need to be disciplined, but these are the most important – once we have this down, the rest will be much easier. The heart is the seat of your emotions, the mind is the seat of your intellect, and your actions are reflective of what you believe in your heart and mind. If you want your life to take a positive turn, you must focus your efforts at personal discipline in these three areas.

The writer of Proverbs was talking, as he often does, about being receptive to God's wisdom – he then gives us this promise:

> *Then you will understand what is right, just, and fair, and you will know how to find the <u>right course of action</u> every time. For wisdom will enter your <u>heart</u>, and <u>knowledge will fill you with joy</u>. Wise <u>planning</u> will watch over you. <u>Understanding</u> will keep you safe.*
> – Proverbs 2:9-11

This covers the three areas of focus that are necessary. When we fill our minds with the things of God, our hearts will be transformed, and our actions will follow the lead of our heart.

> *Don't become so well-adjusted to your culture that you fit into it without even thinking. Instead, fix your attention on God. You'll be changed from the inside out. Readily recognize what he wants from you, and quickly respond to it. Unlike the culture around you, always dragging you down to its level of immaturity, God brings the best out of you, develops well-formed maturity in you.*
> – Romans 12:2 (MSG)

Now the way to begin this process of transformation is to take God's Word and read it, and pray through it, and get to know Him better. And I don't want to just read the Word; I want to experience it, by taking what I have learned and putting it into practice. There is nothing sadder than a person who has lots of head knowledge about God, but doesn't know how to live out the kind of life God's Word has revealed to them. To actually put God's Word into practice I need to be personally disciplined enough that as I read it, I am constantly evaluating my heart against what God has revealed.

For instance, let's say I'm reading through Proverbs and I come across this passage:

> *Do not withhold good from those who deserve it when it's in your power to help them. If you can help your neighbor now, don't say, "Come back tomorrow, and then I'll help you."*
> – Proverbs 3:27-28

Now I'm going to evaluate my life by the Word of God by asking these questions: "Am I withholding from those whom it is in my power to help? Have I been stingy and lacking in generosity?" If the answer is, "Yes, I'm not living up to God's standard" then I need to change that right away and begin to be a generous person.

You see the pattern–I've learned something intellectually–"God wants me to help those I can."–It's affected me emotionally–"God wants me to find those in need" – and it's effected my actions – "Tomorrow, I'm going to give $20.00 to my friend." (Women shelter)

This simple pattern works for our relationships, our moral and ethical values, and every possible area of our lives. <u>Go to God's Wor</u>d, <u>learn what</u> He says, <u>let it transform your heart</u>, and then <u>apply</u> the truth that you've learned – that's all there is to it.

4. DECIDE TO DO THIS RIGHT NOW

There is a fictional story I once heard where Satan called to himself the emissaries of hell and said he wanted to send one of them to earth to aid women and men in the ruination of their souls. He asked which one would want to go. One creature came forward and said, "I will go." Satan said, "If I send you, what will you tell the children of men?" He said, "I will tell the children of men that there is no heaven." Satan said, "They won't believe you, for there is a bit of heaven in every human heart. In the end everyone knows that right and good must have the victory. You may not go." Then another came forward, darker and fouler than the first. Satan said, "If I send you, what will you tell the children of men?" He said, "I will tell them there is no hell." Satan looked at him and said, "Oh, no; they won't believe you, for in every human heart there's a thing called conscience, an inner voice which testifies to the truth that not only will good be triumphant, but that evil will be defeated. You may not go." Then one last creature came forward, this one from the darkest place of all. Satan said to him, "And if I send you, what will you say to women and men to aid them in the destruction of their souls?" He said, "I will tell them there is no hurry." – Satan said, "Go!"

It's a fictional story, but the point finds its basis in reality. I have no doubt that there are some reading this right now thinking, "This personal discipline thing sounds like just what I need. I'll start as soon as…(fill in the blank).

And if that is what you're thinking, you will never get around to this. You need to make a decision right now that you are going to follow through. I can't make your decision for you, and you can't make mine for me. We are each personally responsible for deciding that today is the day that we are going to get on track and begin following God's principles for personal discipline. This is the first step that will take you down the path of spiritual maturity – but you have to make a conscious decision to do it right now.

During the Winter Olympics my wife and I watched the women's skating competition. I looked at her and said, "It's amazing how physically disciplined these women are – they've trained themselves in every possible way, every day, for most of their lives, so that they can compete at this level." What about us? Are we willing to go into spiritual training? Is what God wants from us more important than physical training? More important than the Olympics? Of course it is – now it's up to each of us to start taking the steps necessary, right now.

What kind of friend am I?

Key #5: HOW TO CHOOSE THE RIGHT FRIENDS

[7]On the advice of Dr. Alexander Graham Bell, the parents of Helen Keller, who was both deaf and blind, sent for a teacher from the Perkins Institution for the Blind in Boston, Massachusetts. Anne Sullivan, a 19-year-old orphan, was chosen for the task of instructing 6-year-old Helen. It was the beginning of a close and lifelong friendship between them. By means of a manual alphabet, Anne "spelled" into Helen's hand such words as *doll* or *puppy.* Two years later Helen was reading and writing Braille fluently. At 10 Helen learned different sounds by placing her fingers on her teacher's larynx and "hearing" the vibrations. Later Helen went to Radcliffe College, where Anne spelled the lectures into Helen's hand. After graduating with honors, Helen decided to devote her life to helping the blind and deaf. As part of that endeavor, she wrote many books and articles and traveled around the world making speeches. Since Helen's speeches weren't intelligible to some, Anne often translated them for her.

---

[7] *Helen Keller, The Story of My Life (Doubleday, 1954)*

> Their nearly 50 years of companionship ended when Anne died in 1936. Helen wrote these endearing words about her lifelong friend: "My teacher is so near to me that I scarcely think of myself apart from her. I feel that her being is inseparable from my own, and that the footsteps of my life are in hers. All the best of me belongs to her—there is not a talent or an inspiration or a joy in me that has not been awakened by her loving touch."

What a marvelous testimony of friendship – if we all had friends like that, what a different kind of world we would live in. But the truth is, many of us don't have those kind of friendships, even though we need them desperately to thrive and survive in a world like ours. Thankfully, the book of Proverbs gives us instruction on how to find the right kinds of friends that will be with us through thick and thin. And in just a moment we're going to look at this instruction, but let's begin with:

FRIENDSHIP FACTS:

There are two very basic truths about friends that we need to look at before we go any further with this.

1. You need friends

I know that this is a no-brainer, but some of us need to be reminded that friendship is necessary if we are going to lead a healthy, productive life.

> *Two people can accomplish more than twice as much as one; they get a better return for their labor. If one person falls, the other can reach out and help. But people who are alone when they fall are in real trouble.*
> – Ecclesiastes 4:9-10

His point is not really about labor or help getting up from a fall – his point is that we are in need of companionship. That is true of you, and it is true of me as well.

2. Your choice of friends is critical

What I'm going to say here applies to everyone, no matter what age you are, but this is especially important for those of you who are younger. Who you make friends with today, will at some level, determine what type of future you are going to have. Are the friends you presently have lifting you up, or pulling you down?

> *Whoever walks with the wise will become wise; whoever walks with fools will suffer harm.* – Proverbs 13:20

The walk that he is referring to is the walk of life – the journey that we all take. And who you take with you on that journey is of utmost importance. We all have a choice in life, as to who we are going to spend our time with. We can pick people who are a bad influence and hang out with them and allow them to influence us to go down the tubes with them, or we can make friends with people who will not drag us down into the gutter with them.

Now, I'm not trying to say that God doesn't love these people, but I am trying to make the point that you are going to be <u>influenced</u> by those you <u>spend the most time with</u>, so you better make sure you choose the right kind of people.

THE KIND OF "FRIENDS" TO AVOID

The book of Proverbs tells us some specific things that some people do that God absolutely detests – now it only makes sense that if we meet people who do these things, they are the type of people we should not choose to be our friends.

> *There are six things the LORD hates—no, seven things he detests: haughty eyes, a lying tongue, hands that kill the innocent, a heart that plots evil, feet that race to do wrong, a false witness who pours out lies, a person who sows discord among brothers.*
> – Proverbs 6:16-19

Let's break this down and see what kind of friends we should avoid:

1. People who have a superiority complex – "*haughty eyes*"

The Message paraphrase says, "eyes that are arrogant." This is a person who views him or herself as having great value, but they devalue those around them. "I am smart, you are dumb." – "I went to college, you didn't finish high school." – "I'm a winner, you're a loser." – "I'm a professional, you're a factory worker."

> *Pride goes before destruction, and haughtiness before a fall.*
> – Proverbs 16:18

2. People who are loose with the truth – *"lying tongue"*

These are people who are either out and out

liars, or people who fudge things by telling "little white lies," or frequently exaggerate. Sometimes these folks get so used to lying that they even start to believe the lies that they are telling. And the next thing you know, you're either going to become a part of one of their lies, or even pick up their habit yourself.

3. People who have destructive behavior patterns – *"hands that kill the innocent"*

Now you're probably thinking, *I don't know any murderers, so I'm okay with this one for sure* – but this covers much more than murder in principle. Anyone who violates the weak and the powerless would fall into this category. These are people who push others around; people who take advantage of those who are weaker than they are; and people who pick on the vulnerable. If you hang out with this type of person, it's just a matter of time until you become their next victim.

4. People who are drawn to think and do evil – *"a heart that plots evil, feet that race to do wrong."*

This is a person who plans and justifies evil behavior. This is the person who rationalizes adultery, or who makes a profit through shady dealings with others. This person has been influenced to do things in opposition to God's will and they will do their best to get you to join in their behavior.

5. People who slander and gossip – *"a false witness who pours out lies"*

This sounds a lot like number 2, but there is a big difference. This person tells lies too, but they are lies designed to slander someone else. These are people who are quick to pass on damaging information about someone else, or people who don't keep information confidential. You know what I mean? This is the person who says, "Did you hear about...." and then they go on to spread some vicious rumor about someone else. If you accept this person as your friend, it's just a matter of time until you become the victim or their slander.

6. People who stir up trouble – *"a person who sows discord"*

Do you know of anyone who goes out of his or her way to stir up trouble? This is the kind of person that pits two friends against each other and then sits back and enjoys the battle that takes place.

> *A troublemaker plants seeds of strife;*
> *gossip separates the best of friends.*
> – Proverbs 16:28

These people also tend to be the type that are easily offended by others, but have no problem at all offending everyone around them. They hold grudges, and refuse to forgive those who have wronged them, but expect you to overlook everything they've done wrong. Avoid these types like the plague, or you'll be sorry in the end.

Now we've quickly looked at what type of friends to avoid – we can now take this same list and consider the opposites, and discover:

THE KIND OF FRIENDS TO ACCEPT

Again, before we go any further I'm not talking here about being stuck-up, or cliquish or anything along those lines – I'm talking about building healthy relationships with people who are going to lift you up rather than knock you down.

Because just as the friends to avoid will influence you negatively, the friends God says to accept will influence you in a positive way.

1. People who are humble.

Rather than someone who looks down on you, you need to find someone who has a sense of humility about them – a person who recognizes your personal value.

> *Pride ends in humiliation, while humility brings honor.*
> – Proverbs 29:23

You need someone who looks upon you as a friend, not because of degrees earned, money in the bank, or because you're the best-looking person around. They value you for being you, and that's all that's necessary

2. People who always speak the truth.

If there is one thing I cannot stand, it is a liar – if they're dishonest with what is coming out of their mouths, they're probably dishonest in the way they live their lives.

> *Just as damaging as a mad man shooting a lethal weapon is someone who lies to a friend and then says, "I was only joking."*
> – Proverbs 26:18-19

You need to find a friend who doesn't make stuff up, who doesn't exaggerate, and who doesn't stretch the truth to fit his or her needs. If I have to doubt what someone is telling me based on past experience, I'm never going to know if what they're telling me is true or not – and that is no way to build a relationship.

3. People who are tenderhearted.

This is the person who has a soft spot in their heart for those who are weak, poor, or in some kind of need. This is the person who imitates the compassion of Jesus Christ in the way that they treat others. This is the type of friend that isn't going to desert me when I'm down, but instead is going to lend me a helping hand. *Bart*

4. People who have high integrity.

These are the people who have built their lives on a solid foundation, and by befriending them; your own life and faith will be strengthened. *Cindy, Char, Angel*

> People with integrity have firm footing, but those who follow crooked paths will slip and fall.
> – Proverbs 10:9

As Jazz Saxophonist Charlie Park said, *"If you don't live it, it won't come out of your horn."* I want to make sure that those I choose to be friends with are people who not only preach it, but also live it out in their daily experience.

5. People who are trustworthy.

I need someone as a friend that I can count on – someone who is going to stick by me no matter what happens – someone who I can trust to always be truthful. *Ange, Barb, Kathleen*

> *Friends come and friends go, but a true friend sticks by you like family.*
> – Proverbs 18:24 (MSG)

We need to know that our friends are the kind of people that will never turn their backs on us, and will never turn against us.

6. People who are quick to avoid conflict.

While you don't want friends who aren't willing to deal with problems you have between you, you also want ones who seek peace at all costs.

> *Avoiding a fight is a mark of honor;* *Kathleen*
> *only fools insist on quarreling.* *B - Barb*
> – Proverbs 20:3 *Cindy Char*
> *Jessie*

Rather than trying to sow discord, you need friends who bring harmony into your life and into the relationship you have together.

I am hoping that by simply going through these lists with you, you are able to better evaluate the friendships you presently have. You need to decide if the friends you have now are the kind that God would want you to have, or if they are bringing you down instead. And once you've made that decision you'll be able to know whether you need to keep the friends you have, or get rid of them and find ones that are better for you. It's not really that hard to figure out – they are either helping you or hindering you. Let me leave you with this one thing to remember no matter what situation you find yourself in today – whether you presently have bad friends, good friends, or no friends –remember – **<u>GOD</u> IS THE MOST IMPORTANT FRIEND OF ALL!** You can trust Him to be the perfect friend at all times and in every situation.

Key #6: HOW TO OVERCOME PRIDE

[8]Not long ago, there was a CEO of a Fortune 500 company who pulled into a service station to get gas. He went inside to pay, and when he came out he noticed his wife engaged in a deep discussion with the service station attendant – It turned out that she knew him. In fact back in high school before she met her eventual husband, she used to date this man. The CEO got in the car, and the two drove in silence. He was feeling pretty good about himself when he finally spoke: "I bet I know what you were thinking. I bet you were thinking you're glad you married me, a Fortune 500 CEO, and not him, a service station attendant." "No, I was thinking if I'd married him, he'd be a Fortune 500 CEO and you'd be a service station attendant." Pride can be a very ugly thing, can't it?

As we continue our consideration of *Proverbs for life*, we're going to discover that this topic of pride is one that comes up often in the Bible. It is something that God detests, which means it is

---

[8] *John Ortberg in Love Beyond Reason (Zondervan, 1998), pp. 142-43*

also something that we need to make sure is not a dominant force in our lives. There are three aspects to pride I want us to consider this together:

1. WHAT PRIDE IS

Now, it is important that we understand that there are two different kinds of pride.
The kind that is acceptable to God, we'll just call:

1) The Good Pride

This is the kind of pride that you have in your kids, or when you've finally accomplished something you've worked very hard at. For instance, let's consider these Scriptures:

> *Grandchildren are the crowning glory of the aged; parents are the pride of their children.* – Proverbs 17:6

This is the type of pride that you have in your family – you're glad for them, and their accomplishments – or just proud that you're related to each other. That is a wonderful thing, and there is nothing wrong with it.

Paul wrote to the Church in Corinth and commended them this way:

> *I have the highest confidence in you, and my pride in you is great. You have greatly encouraged me; you have made me happy despite all our troubles.*
> – 2 Corinthians 7:4

Paul had been greatly encouraged by a turn-around in the Corinthian Church and he took great pride in them for their willingness to change their ways. I see no problem in being proud that you did a good job, or that you earned a degree, or that your child placed first in the spelling bee. Those are all great things, and things you should be proud of – that is Good Pride.

2) The Bad Pride

Bad pride is pride that is misplaced – almost without exception; it is pride in oneself that is not justified, or pride used to be condescending toward others. God puts it in a category of character traits that He hates.

> *All who fear the LORD will hate evil. That is why I hate pride, arrogance, corruption, and perverted speech.*
> – Proverbs 8:13

Obviously, if the Lord hates it, it is something

that we want to avoid. But before we learn how to avoid it, let's look at:

2. WHAT "BAD" PRIDE DOES (The 3-Ds)

My fear is that when we talk about a subject like "pride," people won't take it seriously. You think, well it's not adultery, or stealing, or something like that. But as we'll see, the things that pride leads to are very serious indeed.

1) Leads to Disgrace

[9]Newsweek provided this description of the dethroned Saddam Hussein: In a part of the world where pride and dignity mean everything, the images were clearly intended to shame. A nameless doctor or medical technician, wearing rubber gloves, was seen closely examining the man's hair, perhaps looking for vermin. Prodded with a tongue depressor, the man opened his mouth; the doctor peered at the pink flesh of his throat and scraped off a few cells for DNA identification. Then the world saw the man's face – Haggard, defeated meek and weak. The Glorious Leader, Direct Descendant of the

---

[9] *"How We Got Saddam," Newsweek (12-22-03), pp. 23-24*

Prophet, the Lion of Babylon, the Father of the Two Lion Cubs, the Anointed One, the Successor of Nebuchadnezzar, the Modern Saladin of Islam had been brought low, forced to bow down to contemplate his fate while waiting to stand trial.

Saddam Hussein, while perhaps an extreme example, could be the poster boy for this particular downfall of pride. One minute he was the proudest man on earth, and the next he is humiliated before the entire world.

> *Pride leads to disgrace, but with humility comes wisdom.*
> – Proverbs 11:2

If you are a proud person, it is only a matter of time until you're brought down off your high horse. It might be tomorrow, or ten years from now, but it will happen.

> *"For the proud will be humbled, but the humble will be honored."*
> – Luke 14:11

Now, what we want to do, if this is a problem of ours, is take care of it now instead of waiting until we are embarrassed in front of our friends.

2) Leads to Disputes

[10]German orchestra violinists are suing for a pay raise, claiming they play many more notes per concert than their colleagues do. The 16 violinists point to their less-busy colleagues who play flute, oboe, or trombone. The director of the Beethoven Orchestra in Bonn, Laurentius Bonitz, argues that the violinists shouldn't be paid more: "Maybe it's an interesting legal question, but musically, it's very clear to everyone."

The church is like the orchestra – There isn't room for prima donnas or people who think they should be held to a level higher than others.

> *Pride leads to arguments; those who take advice are wise.* – Proverbs 13:10

The arguments that take place come from the fact that those who think they are superior in their pride, cannot get along with those who they feel are "under them."

---

[10] *Violinists Say Pay Far from Noteworthy," Chicago Tribune (3-24-04)*

When you find contention in a group, in a neighborhood, in a church or church group, the basis of it will always be found to be pride.

3) Leads to Discipline

There are a lot of things that God looks past, but pride isn't one of them.

> *The LORD <u>despises</u> pride; be assured that <u>the proud will be punished</u>.*
> – Proverbs 16:5

Now, why would God despise pride? I think there are a number of possibilities, but consider it from this angle. God is perfect in every possible way – a person who sets himself up to be something he is not, is in some ways usurping the place of God in his life.

Let me put it another way – the proud person is not going to see the same need for God in her life, as the humble does, because she thinks she already has it all together. And God says that that kind of person is going to be disciplined by Him. I don't know exactly what form that discipline will take, but I do know that God will follow through on His promise.

Now I know that none of you want to be disgraced, fall into dispute, or be disciplined by God, so let's go to our next section to find the solution:

3. WHAT YOU CAN DO ABOUT IT

There are three very specific things that we can do to rid ourselves of pride:

1) Perform a Reality Check

[11]Chan Gailey, football coach for the Georgia Tech Yellow Jackets, told how he learned a lesson in humility. Gailey was then head coach of Alabama's Troy State, and they were playing for a National Championship. The week before the big game, he was headed to the practice field when a secretary called him back to take a phone call. Somewhat irritated, Gailey told her to take a message because he was on his way to practice. She responded, "But it's Sports Illustrated." – "I'll be right there," he said. As he made his way to the building, he began to think about the upcoming article. It would be great publicity for a small school like Troy State

---

[11] *Chan Gailey speaking at a dinner in Dalton, Georgia (4-20-04)*

to be in Sports Illustrated. As he got closer, he realized that a three-page article wouldn't be sufficient to tell the whole story. Coming even closer to his office, he started thinking that he might be on the cover. – "Should I pose or go with an action shot," he wondered. His head was spinning with all of the possibilities. When he picked up the phone and said hello, the person asked, "Is this Chan Gailey?" – "Yes, it is," he replied confidently. "This is Sports Illustrated, and we're calling to let you know that your subscription is running out. Are you interested in renewing?" Coach Gailey concluded the story by saying, "You are either humble or you will be humbled."

Pride ends in humiliation, while humility brings honor.
– Proverbs 29:23

There is nothing wrong with knowing what you are good at and what you are not good at – in fact, that is true humility. It is when we have a puffed up view of ourselves that we get in trouble. But if you can take an honest inventory of yourself, you'll be fine.

For instance, I know that I'm not going to be asked to be on the cover of GQ. I also know that I'm not going to qualify to be in the MENSA club for people with genius IQs. I know that other people have great ideas, opinions, and so forth. But I also don't think I'm stupid, or that I don't have anything to offer. In fact, I know that God has gifted me in certain areas. And as long as I have a realistic view of who I am and what my place is in this world, I'll display the kind of humility that God is looking for.

2) Humble Yourself Before God

We need to remind ourselves that there is only one God, and we're not Him. When I look at God and see that He is the Creator of the Universe, that He is the One who knows all, and sees all – and that He is perfect in every possible way, it should bring me down to my knees in worship of Him. When I read about Jesus giving Himself on the Cross to literally die in my place, it makes me realize that any sacrifice I can give will pale in comparison. When I really come to know God, and accept Him for who He is, I will have no choice but to bow before Him in fear and reverence.

> *True humility and fear of the LORD lead to riches, honor, and long life.*
> – Proverbs 22:4

I hope you can see God clearly enough to realize that you are compelled to humble yourself before Him. If you're not there yet, I pray that you get there soon – read the Word of God, pray without ceasing, search Him out with your every moment.

God will make Himself known to you, and when He does, you will see what I'm talking about very, very clearly, and then your life will be changed.

3) Review, Repent, Renew

Like most areas where we seek spiritual growth, this is an ongoing process. I wish I could push a button that would take all of the bad pride out of my life forever, but it just doesn't work that way. Just like you, I find the ugly head of pride rearing itself up in my life at the most inopportune times. And I've come to realize that I have to constantly work on this, but with God's help, I know it can be overcome.

Periodically I have to review my life, repent where I've allowed pride to take hold, and ask God to bring me through the process of renewal where I draw closer to Him, by pushing myself out of the way.

> *Don't be impressed with your own wisdom. Instead, <u>fear the LORD</u> and <u>turn your back on evil</u>. Then <u>you will gain renewed health and vitality</u>.*
> – Proverbs 3:7-8

There are the three steps right there in that passage – Review, Repent, and Renew. Can you do that? I'm confident that you can.

As we close this chapter, I want to ask you to do yourself a favor in this area sometime today or within the next couple of days. Ask your spouse, or a close, trusted friend, if you exhibit this bad type of pride we've been talking about in your life. Ask them to be completely honest with you, and when they are, don't get mad at them.

Because sometimes in this particular area, we don't see it in ourselves as well as those around us might. And if you discover that this is a problem, it's time to - - Perform a Reality Check – Humble yourself before God – Review, Repent, and Renew.

Key #7: HOW TO GUARD AGAINST GOSSIP

[12]In Today's Christian Woman, Ramona Cramer Tucker writes: My friend Michelle admits to being caught in a nasty situation. While at a restaurant over lunch, Michelle and her coworker, Sharon, stopped in the restroom to fix their makeup before returning to their jobs. Their small talk turned to the subject of who drove them crazy. Immediately Michelle launched into a two-minute diatribe about Beth, a mutual coworker. As Michelle prepared to divulge more specifics, a stall door opened. Out walked Beth, red-faced and angry. In a split second, what had seemed like a pressure-relief session turned into an awkward mess. Michelle and Beth stared at each other in embarrassed panic. Michelle knew she couldn't take her words back. In the instant their eyes met, Beth fled out the door.

That afternoon, Beth didn't return to work, and the next day Michelle heard

---

[12] Ramona Cramer Tucker, "Loose Lips," Christian Reader (March / April 2002), pp.38-39

through the grapevine that Beth had resigned. While other staff members openly cheered what seemed to be good news, Michelle felt miserable. She wished she had talked *to* Beth instead of talking *about* Beth. Although that situation happened five years ago, Michelle's never forgotten it. She tried to reach Beth several times by phone, then wrote her a letter of apology, but Beth never responded. Michelle says she, too, learned her lesson about loose lips the hard way. What's worse is that Michelle's a Christian, and Beth, to her knowledge, isn't.

What side of that story did you immediately relate to? Michelle's or Beth's? Now I don't want to waste anybody's time, so if you don't relate to either side – if you don't have a struggle with gossip yourself, or if you've never been hurt by gossipers, you're free to move on. But if you've found yourself being a gossip or if you've ever felt the sting from someone gossiping about you, then dig in because God has something to say to us. In this chapter we'll deal with the problem from Michelle's perceptive–the problem of being a gossip, because if we can solve that problem, the other will be solved also.

1. UNDERSTAND WHAT GOSSIP IS

Let me give you the dictionary definition: 1) *Rumor or talk of a personal, sensational, or intimate nature;* 2) *A person who habitually spreads intimate or private rumors or facts.*

It almost always has to do with talking about someone else behind their back, in a way you wouldn't if they were present with you. And while sometimes what they say is untrue or exaggerated, it might very well be the truth, but told in a way meant to hurt the other person. It can even be done by putting the point of emphasis on a particular word, or by raising an eyebrow while telling the story.

For instance, I might tell you: "Did you know that John and Beth bought a new house?" Or I might say, "Did *you know* that John and Beth bought a *new* house?" And most of the time it is much worse than that – I might say, "Harry and Sue are having marital problems again. What is wrong with those people"? But if I ran into Harry and Sue on the street I might say, "Hey how's everything going with you guys? Good to see you again." As I've mentioned, sometimes people tell out and out lies to hurt others.

So those are some examples of what gossip is, and the intention of it is always to harm the other person, whether the person doing the gossiping thinks of it that way or not.

2. RECOGNIZE GOSSIP'S DESTRUCTIVE POWER

Coming out of church one Sunday, Mrs. Smith asked her husband, "Do you think that Johnson girl is tinting her hair?" "I didn't even see her," admitted Mr. Smith. "And that dress Mrs. Jones was wearing," continued Mrs. Smith, "Really, don't tell me you think that's the proper outfit for a mother of two." "I'm afraid I didn't notice that either," said Mr. Smith. "Oh, for heaven's sake," snapped Mrs. Smith. "A lot of good it does you to go to church."

Have you ever been around someone like that? It's kind of funny when it is just a joke that we tell, but when it is for real the consequences aren't so humorous. I really don't think most people take this issue seriously enough. This is one of those sins we tend to look past and say it isn't that big of a deal. But the truth is, it is a huge deal and it has destroyed many people.

Let's look to the Bible and we'll consider a few together:

1) Gossip Destroys Friendships

A troublemaker plants seeds of strife; gossip separates the best of friends.
– Proverbs 16:28

✻ Donna + David

You start gossiping about your friends, and you won't have those friends for long. In fact, another passage in Proverbs warns us against even associating with a gossip:

A gossip tells secrets, so don't hang around with someone who talks too much. – Proverbs 20:19

Gossips destroy their lives, the lives of their friends and the lives of the people they talk about. How anyone could expect to go around bad-talking someone else, and remain friends with them is beyond me, but they are out there in droves.

2) Gossip Destroys Character

When I gossip to you, I either plant a negative idea in your mind about someone else or I confirm a suspicion you're having. Even if you argue with me and tell me I'm wrong about someone, my words will linger in your mind and create some doubt. And if I involve 3 or 4 other people in my gossip, before you know it, we've become a majority opinion. Our gossip can become the accepted sentiment of someone's character.

> *What dainty morsels rumors are — but they sink deep into one's heart.*
> – Proverbs 18:8

Gossip is a big deal – our words sink deep into someone else's heart. Suddenly, a passing thought becomes someone's reality.

3) Gossip Destroys Trust

Once I find out that you have gossiped about me, or you find out I've gossiped about you, what happens to our relationship? We no longer can trust each other.

> *A gossip goes around revealing secrets, but those who are trustworthy can keep a confidence.*
> – Proverbs 11:13

Perhaps you've heard the saying: *Whoever gossips to you will gossip about you.* Whenever I'm around someone who gossips a lot, I begin to think, "I wonder what they're saying about me?" and I don't think I'm being paranoid either.

The tongue is a small thing, but what enormous damage it can do. A tiny spark can set a great forest on fire.
– James 3:5

The tongue can heal or the tongue can hurt – With it we can boost or burden. The words that we say can either be a load or a lift. They can give comfort or consternation. The words that we speak are very powerful. And we need to remember that once something has come out of our mouths, we can never retrieve it or stop it from doing its damage – it's too late.

3. PARTICIPATE IN A RIGHTEOUS ALTERNATIVE

Perhaps I am idealistic, but I actually believe we can choose not to gossip. And in fact, since the Bible says that gossip is wrong, I have to believe that God can give us the power to not participate in it. Let me give you a few ways to stop gossip in its tracks.

1) Repent

If you have been engaged in this behavior, and I imagine most of us have at some level at some time, we need to repent of it. Consider what happened to Billy Graham and his reaction to it.

In March 2002 more tapes from the days of Richard Nixon were released. On one tape, Billy Graham was heard telling President Richard Nixon that Jews had a "stranglehold" on the American media, which needed to be broken because it was controlling the country. When the tapes were made public, Graham apologized for his remarks. He didn't deny them, but said he couldn't recall making them. Though many people were shocked, no one considers Billy Graham a bigot.

Most people will forgive Graham because of his spotless record, and because he owned up to what he did and asked forgiveness. When we have been caught up in gossip we need to repent, which means we are not only sorry for what we have done, but we are going to stop doing it.

> *Fire goes out for lack of fuel, and quarrels disappear when gossip stops.*
> – Proverbs 26:20

The first line of defense in changing this behavior is to change yourself.

2) Think T.H.I.N.K.

Think T.H.I.N.K. means that you incorporate the following acrostic into your life before you say anything about anyone else. We want to make sure that the words that we say about others are words that God would approve of, and that the person we are talking about would approve of also. It is not always wrong to talk about others, and sometimes it is good and necessary, but we need to make sure what we say fits into the T.H.I.N.K. principle.

T – is it true?
H – is it helpful?
I – is it inspirational?
N – is it necessary?
K – is it kind?

If what we say fits into these simple criteria then it definitely is not gossip. I know that it is difficult to think through all of this every time you say something, but if you start doing it for a while it will begin to flow naturally.

3) Hold Others Accountable

Once you've gotten your own act together, you need to try to help others. I honestly think gossip is one of the most detrimental problems that takes place in the church and society as a whole, and we all need to do our part to stop it.

> *"If another believer sins against you, go privately and point out the fault. If the other person listens and confesses it, you have won that person back."*
> – Matthew 18:15

This text can apply to someone gossiping about you, as well as it does to any other situation. Go to that person and ask, "Have you been saying this about me?" If they admit it, tell them that you do not want them to do it anymore, and hopefully they will repent and stop doing it. If you hear someone else gossiping about another person, try one of these questions: "Can I quote you on this?" or "Have you talked to [that person] about this?" Another way you can deal with it, is instead of joining in with the person, think of an admirable quality of the person being talked about and say, "You know, what I like most about [that person] is. . ."

I'd like to conclude this chapter with some very wise words from James that I think are a good reminder for us:

> *A bit in the mouth of a horse controls the whole horse. A small rudder on a huge ship in the hands of a skilled captain sets a course in the face of the strongest winds. A word out of your mouth may seem of no account, but it*

can accomplish nearly anything — or destroy it! It only takes a spark, remember, to set off a forest fire. A careless or wrongly placed word out of your mouth can do that. By our speech we can ruin the world, turn harmony to chaos, throw mud on a reputation, send the whole world up in smoke and go up in smoke with it, smoke right from the pit of hell. – James 3:3-6 (MSG)

Key #8: HOW TO EXPERIENCE PROSPERITY

Several men in the locker room of a private exercise club were talking when a cell phone lying on the bench rang. One man picked it up without hesitation, and the following conversation ensued: "Hello?" – "Honey, It's me." – "Sugar!" "I'm at the mall two blocks from the club. I saw a beautiful mink coat. It is absolutely gorgeous! Can I buy it? It's only $1,500." "Well, okay, if you like it that much."

"Thanks! Oh, I also stopped by the Mercedes dealership and saw the new models. I saw one I really liked. I spoke with the salesman, and he gave me a great price." "How much?" – "Only $60,000!" – "Okay, but for that price I want it with all the options." "Great! Before we hang up, there's something else. It might seem like a lot, but, well, I stopped by to see the real estate agent this morning, and I saw the house we had looked at last year. It's on sale! Remember? The beachfront property with the pool and the English garden?" "How much are they asking?" "Only $450,000, a great price, and we have that much in the bank to cover it." "Well then, go ahead and buy it, but put in a bid for only $420,000, okay?" "Okay, sweetie. Thanks! I'll see you later! I love you!" – "I love you, too." The man hung up, closed the phone's flap, and raised it up, asking, "Does anyone know who this cell phone belongs to?"

Wouldn't it be nice to really be able to make those decisions so easily? Or maybe it wouldn't – I think it would depend a lot on our personal character. When we talk about prosperity, specifically financial prosperity, I think there is a lot of confusion for us as to what the Bible says. On the one hand you have some TV preachers telling you that God wants everyone to be rich, and if you're not, you don't have faith in God. Then on the other hand, you have some who say that God wants everyone to be poor, and that we should feel some sense of guilt for being materially well off.

What we discover in the book of Proverbs is somewhere in between those two extremes – God specifically gives us the principles for becoming prosperous, but He also tells us to pursue prosperity in a godly way. In other words, God encourages us to pursue wealth, as long as we don't forget Him in the process. Let's get into this and you'll see what I mean.

1. PURSUE WISDOM IN EVERY WAY

Of course, *Wisdom* is the theme of the entire book

of Proverbs, and we find the merits of pursuing it applied to every possible subject, including prosperity. Let's look at a couple of verses together:

> *Those who <u>listen to instruction</u> will <u>prosper</u>; those who trust the LORD will be happy.* – Proverbs 16:20

> *To <u>acquire wisdom</u> is to love oneself; people who <u>cherish understanding</u> will <u>prosper</u>.* – Proverbs 19:8

There are several important actions listed in these verses we need to be involved in if we are to experience prosperity, and they all have to do with our minds. We need to acquire wisdom, cherish understanding, and listen to instruction. Now these things can happen through a variety of experiences, but they mainly have to do with gaining an intellectual and spiritual education.

Let's say that I plan on becoming prosperous through owning an advertising business. Most likely, I'm going to need to receive instruction in this area from others who have been successful at it. I might need to go to college and get a degree in this area. I might need to work for someone else who is successful for a while, learn everything I can, and later start my own business.

There are no shortcuts to this – I need to learn how to be wise in business dealings, how to treat my customers, my suppliers, and 1,000 other things that will be involved in being successful. In other words, if I am going to be prosperous I need to take the advice of Proverbs to heart and do whatever is necessary to be educated in a particular area.

And while there are people who are prosperous who never spent a day in a college classroom, I will guarantee you they got educated somewhere – through an apprenticeship, through books, through on-the-job-training. Somewhere along the way, they had enough diligence to do what was necessary to succeed, and if you want to succeed in this way, you'll need to do the same.

2. BE GENEROUS WITH ALL YOU HAVE

[13] A guy named Joel Schelsinger borrowed a book from his local library in Orchard Park, NY. But by the time Joel revisited the library to return the book, it was 24 years later. He had borrowed *The Joy of*

What about people who do not deserve it

[13] *Uh, I Found This in My Attic,"The Christian Science Monitor (5-20-05)*

Camping in 1981, but forgotten about it. In 2005, now living in another state, Joel had rediscovered the volume and determined to make things right. Traveling 400 miles to his old hometown, Joel returned the book and paid a fine of $2,190. The maximum penalty for overdue or lost books is $15 – Joel wasn't satisfied with that. Knowing that the Orchard Park library faced a budget crunch, Joel calculated what his actual fine would be at 10-cents-a-day for all those years. It added up to $2,190. Referring to his over-and-above act of generosity, Joel said, "I hope they can do some good things with it; maybe buy some books." Now here's a guy who could have paid the minimum, or never even returned the book, and no one would have been the wiser – but he had a generous spirit.

The generous prosper and are satisfied; those who refresh others will themselves be refreshed.
– Proverbs 11:25

One of the secrets to prosperity is personal generosity. It is amazing how even secular books on business and success follow this biblical principle and I'm not even sure they are aware that it is in the Bible. I've even heard completely secular and successful people use the term "tithe" in reference to giving a large portion of their earnings to non-profit organizations. It is a spiritual principle of success that many of us miss. And while I would not give for the purpose of receiving, at the same time I know that God says that He will give a return on my generous investment toward those who are in need.

Don't expect to receive from God, if you do not give for God. When the offering plate is passed each Sunday, don't let it pass you by without dropping any money in it and then go home and ask God to bless your finances. And I'm not talking about just being generous to the church, but being a person who lives a generous life, and gives of their time, and finances to those in need.

> *Whoever gives to the poor will lack nothing. But a curse will come upon those who close their eyes to poverty.*
> – Proverbs 28:27

One of the legitimate reasons a godly person should seek prosperity is so he or she can share the wealth with others who don't have it. If it weren't for wealthy Christians who were generous in giving their money to foreign missions, orphanages, schools, and many other ventures, we wouldn't be able to accomplish nearly what is being accomplished today.

3. LIVE FOR RIGHTEOUSNESS

Now I want to make sure we're real cautious when we talk about prosperity. Because there are some of us who just can't handle it, because we will be seduced by the money, and will quit living the life of righteousness God calls us to.

> *For <u>the love of money is at the root of all kinds of evil</u>. And some people, craving money, have wandered from the faith and pierced themselves with many sorrows.* – 1 Timothy 6:10

Notice that he doesn't say "money is evil" but the "<u>love</u> of money" is evil. If the pursuit of financial success gets in the way of your pursuit of God, you're walking down the wrong path, so we need to be very careful with this. And God says that He will not help you prosper if you turn from Him.

> *The crooked heart will not prosper; the twisted tongue tumbles into trouble.*
> – Proverbs 17:20

That doesn't mean you can't prosper, but God isn't going to be the one driving it, so guess who is? Let's just say it's somebody you don't want to align yourself with.

So you need to ask yourself some questions as you pursue success:

*Am I more concerned about what God thinks of me, or what my colleagues think of me?

*Am I spending more time thinking up plans to make more money, or more time meditating on the things of God?

*Am I willing to cross ethical and moral lines to get ahead, or am I making sure I am completely honest in everything that I do?

*Am I pursuing prosperity so that I can better serve God, or so that I can get along okay without Him?

Those some of the questions I would ask; maybe you can think of some more. The point is that I do not want to lose the God who owns everything in my pursuit of a small portion of His holdings.

4. WORK HARD AND PLAN WELL

This is something a lot of people like to avoid, but the fact is you cannot be prosperous without these two ingredients. You've heard that old saying, "You've got to plan your work and work your plan." That is absolutely true for anyone who wants to be successful.

Too many of us are like the farmer who went out to gather eggs. As he walked across the farmyard toward the hen house, he noticed the pump was leaking – So he stopped to fix it. It needed a new washer, so he set off to the barn to get one. But on the way he saw that the hayloft needed straightening, so he went off to fetch the pitchfork. Hanging next to the pitchfork was a broom with a broken handle. "I must make a note to myself to buy a new broom handle the next time I go to town," he thought. By now it is clear the farmer is not going to get his eggs gathered, nor is he likely to accomplish anything else he sets out to do. He is utterly, gloriously spontaneous, but he is hardly free. He is, if anything, a prisoner to his unbridled spontaneity. The fact of the matter is that hard work, planning, and personal discipline is the only way to become prosperous in any endeavor.

Listen to these verses from Proverbs:

> *Hard work means prosperity; only fools idle away their time.*
> – Proverbs 12:11

> *Lazy people want much but get little, but those who work hard will prosper and be satisfied.* – Proverbs 13:4

> *Good planning and hard work lead to prosperity, but hasty shortcuts lead to poverty.* – Proverbs 21:5

Now unless you have a big inheritance coming, I promise you that you are not going to become prosperous by luck, or by sitting on your tail end and hoping for it. God says that if you want to be prosperous, make your plan and then get to work. No excuses, no procrastination…just do it.

5. TRUST IN THE LORD WITH ALL YOUR HEART

Maybe I should have started with this one, but I thought it might be better as a reminder at the end. In everything we do, we have to continually put our trust in the Lord. I don't know where you are at right now financially. Some of you might be on the verge of declaring bankruptcy, and others might have so much money you don't know what to do with it. Others might have been doing everything I've mentioned so far but you don't feel real prosperous just yet. Consider this passage of Scripture:

> *Greed causes fighting; trusting the LORD leads to prosperity.*
> – Proverbs 28:25

No matter how bleak your situation looks right now, you've got to keep believing that God knows what is best and He will do whatever is necessary by His own timetable whether we understand it or not. And I also think trusting in the Lord forces us to redefine what we mean by prosperity, because the truth of the matter is, compared to much of the world, everyone reading this is already extremely prosperous.

As I think I've made clear, I don't see anything wrong in seeking success, and even seeking material comfort, but while were doing that, let's not forget that the God we're trusting for the future has been taking care of us in the past. No matter what happens, we need to remember that God has proven Himself trustworthy, so we will continue to place our faith in Him no matter what.

THANK YOU FOR INVESTING IN THIS BOOK!

We'd love to hear your feedback. Please stop by and leave a review at:
http://www.amazon.com/author/barrydavis .
You can also check out our other books there.

If you'd like to see some of our many resources for Bible Study leaders and Pastors, please go to:
http://www.pastorshelper.com

I hope to hear from you soon! May God bless you as you continue to serve Him.

In Christ,

Barry L. Davis

Made in the USA
San Bernardino, CA
21 January 2014